Contents

Minimum System Requirements

Windows
Windows 98 and later, including Windows XP
Pentium Processor, 350 MHZ or higher
128 MB of available RAM
8X CD-ROM
Monitor: thousands of colors, 800 X 600 display, 1024 X 768 recommended
Internet connection: 56K Modem speed or faster
Browser: Netscape 6.1 or IE 5.0 and later
Microphone
Text editor or word processing program

Mac
Mac OS 9.2 and later, including OS10.3
PowerMac or PowerPC G3 or higher
128 MB of available RAM
8X CD-ROM
Monitor: thousands of colors, 800 X 600 display, 1024 X 768 recommended
Internet connection: 56K Modem speed or faster
Browser: Netscape 6.1 or IE 5.0 and later, or Safari 1.x
Microphone
Text editor or word processing program

Introduction

Welcome to the Multimedia CD-ROM 1.0 to accompany *¿Cómo se dice ...?*, Eighth Edition by Jarvis, Lebredo and Mena-Ayllón.

The goal of this Multimedia CD-ROM is to reinforce the concepts covered by each chapter of the textbook by providing additional practice in a self-paced environment. Each chapter includes all or some combination of these five program segments:

- Vocabulario • Estructuras • Pronunciacion • Applicacion • Video • Juegos (crosswords, timed word searches, space invader word association games, word completion maze games)

Knowledge of chapter subject matter is assessed through multiple combinations of question types:

- Fill-in exercises
- Drag and drop activities that include matching, sorting, ordering, or labeling tasks
- True or False questions
- Multiple choice activities
- Short answer or essay questions
- Record-your-response exercises (in response to audio, visual, or text questions)

In addition, the CD-ROM provides supplementary reference material including:

- Glossaries • Verb Charts • Grammar References

Access to additional resources include:

- A link to Smarthinking, Houghton Mifflin's live, online, text-specific tutoring service for students.
- A link to the Houghton Mifflin textbook-specific Web site

Figure 1:
Welcome Screen

Launching the Program

Windows:

1. Insert the CD-ROM into your disk drive.
2. Double click **My Computer** on your desktop.
3. Double click on the CD-ROM icon in **My Computer**.
4. Double click on the Flash icon to launch the CD-ROM.

Macintosh:

1. Insert the CD-ROM into your disk drive.
2. Double click on the CD-ROM icon on your desktop.
3. Double click on the Flash icon to launch the CD-ROM.

How to Use the HMCo World Language CD-ROM
Welcome Screen

You are now ready to begin a study session. Each time you start the program, you will need to enter your name (first name is OK). If you would like to send the scored results of the exercises to your professor (or anyone else), enter their e-mail address in the space provided. Note: This e-mail address will be automatically entered in the *To:* field when you launch your e-mail application from the exercise screens. Click the **Login** button to proceed.

Main Menu

The **Main Menu** *(Figure 2: Main Menu)* is the primary navigation for chapter exercises on the CD-ROM. It also provides access to the **Chapter Menu** as well as various supplemental sections of the CD-ROM, such as **Reference**, **WWW** (which gives you access to the text-book-specific Web site and the *Smarthinking* online tutorial program), **About**, and **Help**.

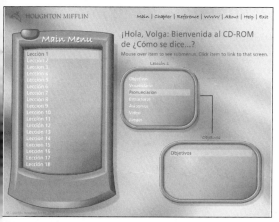

Figure 2:
Main Menu

Mouse-over a chapter title in the Personal Digital Assistant (PDA) to see the core segments within each chapter. The segment titles within each chapter appear in a window to the right of the PDA.

As you mouse-over the segment titles in the segment menu, lesson topics within that segment are revealed in the window below.

To go to the first exercise in either a segment or a specific lesson topic, simply mouse-over the chapter or segment and click to jump to the first exercise.

Chapter Menu

Clicking on a chapter title in the **Main Menu** PDA (or clicking on **Chapter** in the top navigation bar) takes you to the **Chapter Menu** *(Figure 3: Chapter Menu)*. The **Chapter Menu** works similarly to the **Main Menu**. To reveal lesson topics, mouse-over items and click to go to the first exercise in the highlighted item.

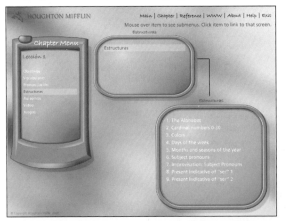

Figure 3:
Chapter Menu

Exercise Screens

The Exercise Screens (*Figure 4: Sample Exercise Screen*) are accessed from either the **Main Menu** or the **Chapter Menu.** The exercises appear as pop-up screens on top of the menus. At any point, you can return to any menu by closing the pop-up screen, by clicking the menu behind the exercise screen, or by clicking the desired menu in the top navigation bar. You can move to the next or previous **Exercise** or **Topic** by clicking the right or left arrows.

At the bottom of the exercise screen there are several additional buttons. Hold your mouse over these buttons to see a description of their function.

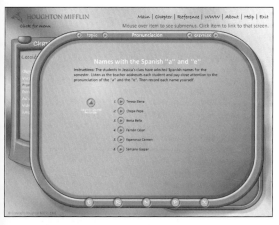

Figure 4: Sample Exercise Screen

- **E** button: launches your default e-mail application. If you do not have a default e-mail application on your computer, you will have to install and set one up to use this function.

- **R** button: opens up your **Progress Report.** This report reflects what you have accomplished so far in your CD-ROM study session.

- **N** button: pops up a blank page, allowing you to take notes from within the program. You can also save these **Notes** to your Hard Drive.

- **P** button: prints the current screen.

- **X** button: exits the exercise screen (Click **Exit** in the navigation bar at the top of the page to exit the program).

Progress Report

The **Progress Report** *(Figure 5: Progress Report)* can be launched from any exercise screen by clicking the **R** button. The **Progress Report** lists all exercises in the chapter. For the exercises you have worked on, it shows the number of questions completed within an exercise, the number of attempts, your score, and your answers to open-ended questions (seen by clicking on the **Data** button). From the **Progress Report**, you can return to any exercise for further practice by clicking the exercise title.

Click the **P** button at the bottom the **Progress Report** screen to print out the displayed **Progress Report** screen. This program prints one screen at a time so you may have to print, scroll down, and print again to print the entire report.

To print the full **Progress Report**, e-mail it, or save it as a file, click the **T** button at the bottom of the **Progress Report** screen. This will launch a new screen with a text version of the report.

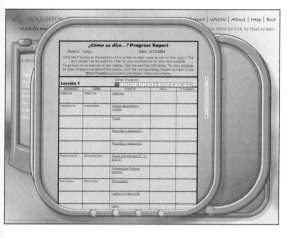

Figure 5:
Progress Report

Progress Report Text Output

The **Progress Report Text** *(Figure 6: Progress Report Text)* screen is a complete version of the **Progress Report** that can be saved to a file. It can then be easily printed, e-mailed as an attachment to your professor, or saved for your own records.
To save your **Progress Report** to a file:

- Select the text you want to save if it is not already selected.
- Copy the selected text (Windows: Control + C; MAC: Command + C)
- Click the **S** (**Save**) button at the bottom of the screen and follow the prompts to save the report to a file.

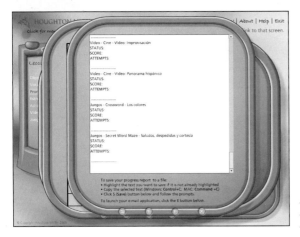

Figure 6:
Progress
Report Text

To launch your e-mail application, click the **E** button at the bottom of the
Progress Report Text screen.

Reference

Clicking the **Reference** label in the top navigation bar launches the **Reference** section
(*Figure 7: Reference*) of the CD. This section opens in a Web browser and you must have
a browser application installed on your computer to use this feature. You may search for
specific words on a page by using the **Find** feature in your browser's main menu. This
section also has information about how to type special characters on your computer keyboard.

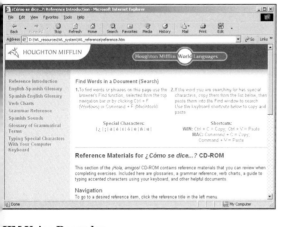

Figure 7:
Reference

HM Voice Recorder

The **Houghton Mifflin Voice Recorder** is used to record your voice to practice speaking a new language.

- Make sure your microphone is plugged in and turned on.
- Click the **Input** button and choose your microphone as the input source.
- Voice recognition systems may interfere with recording. If so, shut them off and restart your computer.
- Click on the red **Record** button to begin recording, and click on the yellow **Stop** button when you are finished. Listen to your recording using the green **Play** button.

- If your voice comes out too quiet or too loud, try adjusting the recording volume level using the slider. This only adjusts the recording sensitivity. To adjust the playback volume, use your operating system's volume control or turn up the volume on your speakers.

- Clicking on the **Record** button a second time will erase your first recording, so be sure to save first.

- A floppy disk will not have sufficient space to save sound files. You must use your hard disk or a larger removable disk format.

- If you launch the **HM Voice Recorder** on the Macintosh and then click the main screen, the recorder will disappear behind the main application. Just click the **Launch Recorder** button a second time to bring it to the front.

Troubleshooting

Sluggish Video Play and Other Performance Issues

If video plays poorly on your computer or you have other performance issues, close the application, restart your computer, close any additional windows or applications, and relaunch the **World Languages CD**. If that does not help, try the application on a faster computer.

Printing a Screen

This program prints what is on the screen. If you wish to print a longer document, you will have to print a screen, scroll down to new data, and print a second screen. Or, if you are printing the **Progress Report**, you can save that to a file, and print out the file.

Video and Subtitles Not Clear

The recommended resolution for this program is 1024 x 768. If your monitor is set at a lower resolution, go to Settings (Windows) or System Preferences (Macintosh) and increase your resolution.

Inserting Special Characters

To insert special characters, click on a character on the special character keypad. The character will be inserted at the end of the last text you have typed. Also see **Typing Special Characters With Your Computer Keyboard** in the **Reference** section (accessible via the top navigation bar).

Reference Section Does Not Appear

If you click **Reference** and it does not appear or appears and then disappears, it may simply be behind the main application. Use Alt > Tab (Windows) or Command > F (Mac) to select the correct window to view.

Mac: Copy and Paste from CD-ROM Exercises Loses Accents

On the Macintosh, you cannot copy and paste directly from one of the exercise windows into an e-mail or word processor or you will lose all the accented characters. To retain the accented characters, copy and paste text from the exercise window into the **Notes** page, and then save the note as directed (The **Notes** function is accessed by clicking the **N** button on the bottom of every exercise screen).

Problems Saving Text from Notes and Progress Report

To save text from **Notes** or the **Progress Report Text** screen, you must select the text you want, copy the text (Control + C on WIN; Command + C on MAC), then click the **S** (**Save**) button at the bottom of the screen. You can only save the **Progress Report** from its text screen. Click **T** (**Text Output**) button at the bottom of the display version of the **Progress Report** to view the text screen.

Trouble Launching Email with E Button

If clicking the **E** button (**Email**) on the exercise screen fails launch your email program, first check that you have a default email client installed. If so, return to the desktop (Control + F for WIN; Command + F for MAC) and launch your email program as you would normally.

Technical Support

For technical support, call Houghton Mifflin Software Support at
1-800-732-3223 between 9 a.m. and 5 p.m. EST Monday through Friday
or e-mail support@hmco.com.

Windows® System Requirements:		Macintosh® System Requirements:	
Operating System:	Windows 95 (with latest updates) and later, including XP	Operating System:	MacOS 8.6(with Carbon Lib), or later, inclu
RAM:	64 MB, 128MB recommended	RAM:	128MB
Processor:	Pentium (or better)	Processor:	PowerMac or PowerPC
Sound:	Sound card, speakers, microphone	Sound:	Sound card, speakers, microphone
Monitor:	600 x 800, 1024 x 786 recommended	Monitor:	600 x 800, 1024 x 786 recommended
Recommended color setting/palette:	32 bit or True color	Recommended color setting/palette:	thousands of colors

HOUGHTON MIFFLIN COMPANY LICENSE AGREEMENT

Before opening this package, you should carefully read the following questions and answers regarding your use of the enclosed product. Opening the package indicates your acceptance of the terms as contained in the answers. If you do not agree with them, you should return the package unopened and your money will be refunded.

Q: WHAT DOES THIS PRODUCT INCLUDE?
A: This product includes compact or floppy disks; software recorded on the disks; contents delivered by the software; and printed documentation.

Q: HOW MAY I USE THIS PRODUCT?
A: You may use the product as follows:
- You may only copy the software onto a single computer for use on that computer and you may only make one archival copy of the software for backup purposes only.
- You may print, transmit or modify the contents only for your individual use and use in the classroom. The product identifies any contents owned by rights holders other than Houghton Mifflin Co you may only use those contents in accordance with current copyright law.
- You may not remove or obscure any copyright, trademark, proprietary rights, disclaimer, or warning notice included on or embedded in any part of the product.
- You may not reverse compile, reverse assemble, reverse engineer, or modify the software, or merge any portion of the software into another computer program.

Q: MAY I USE THE PRODUCT ON MORE THAN ONE COMPUTER?
A: You may use the product on more than one computer as long as there is no possibility that two different people will use the product on two different computers at the same time. If you want to u uct on more than one computer at a time, you must purchase separate copies for each computer location. If you represent an institution intending to use the product in an instructional computer lab to the networking provisions below.

Q: MAY I USE THE PRODUCT ON A NETWORK?
A: If you have purchased multiple licenses for the product, you may provide access to the product via your network (rather than copying the software onto a certain number of computers) as long as reasonable mechanism in place to ensure that the number of persons using the product concurrently does not exceed the number of licenses you have purchased.

Q: WHO OWNS THE PRODUCT?
A: You own the disc on which the software and the contents are recorded. Houghton Mifflin Company grants you a license to use the software and its contents in accordance with the terms and condit in this License Agreement. Houghton Mifflin Company and its licensors own and retain all title, copyright, trademark, and other proprietary rights in and to the software and its contents.

Q: MAY I GIVE THE PRODUCT TO ANOTHER PERSON?
A: You may transfer your license to use the product to another person as long as you permanently transfer the entire product (including all discs, all copies of the software program and all documenta in this package) without keeping a copy for yourself. To transfer your license properly, the recipient must first agree to the terms and conditions of this License Agreement. You may not otherwise license rent, or lease the product without permission from Houghton Mifflin Company.

Q: WHAT CAN I DO IF THE PRODUCT IS DEFECTIVE?
A: Within 30 days of purchase, contact Houghton Mifflin College Software at 800-732-3223 or email: support@hmco.com. They will provide you with shipping instruction for the return and replacement tive disc. Provided the disc has not been physically damaged, Houghton Mifflin Company will replace the defective disc.
- LIMITED WARRANTY. EXCEPT AS STATED ABOVE, HOUGHTON MIFFLIN COMPANY MAKES NO WARRANTIES, EITHER EXPRESS OR IMPLIED, INCLUDING WITHOUT LIMITATION ANY WARRANTY OF MERCHA FITNESS FOR A PARTICULAR PURPOSE.
- REMEDY. Your sole remedy is the replacement of a defective disc, as provided above.
- LIMITATION OF LIABILITY. IN NO EVENT SHALL HOUGHTON MIFFLIN COMPANY OR ANYONE ELSE WHO HAS BEEN INVOLVED IN THE CREATION, PRODUCTION, OR DELIVERY OF THE PRODUCT BE LIABL ANY DIRECT, INCIDENTAL, OR CONSEQUENTIAL DAMAGES, SUCH AS, BUT NOT LIMITED TO, LOSS OF ANTICIPATED PROFITS, BENEFITS, USE, OR DATA RESULTING FROM THE USE OF THE PRODUCT, OR A OF ANY BREACH OF ANY WARRANTY.
- OTHER RIGHTS. Some states do not permit exclusion of implied warranties or exclusion of incidental or consequential damages. The above exclusions may not apply to you. This warranty provides specific legal rights. There may be other rights that you may have which vary from state to state.

Q: ARE THERE ANY RESTRICTIONS ON GOVERNMENT USE OF THE PRODUCT?
A: Houghton Mifflin Company provides this product to government agencies with restricted rights. Restrictions on government use, duplication and disclosure are set forth in subparagraph (c)(1)(ii) of Technical Data and Computer Software clause at DFARS 252.227-7013 and subparagraph (c)(1) and (2) of the Commercial Computer Software - Restricted Rights clause at FAR 52-227-19.

Q: IF I HAVE QUESTIONS ABOUT THIS LICENSE AGREEMENT, WHO MAY I CONTACT?
A: If you have any questions about this License Agreement, you may call Houghton Mifflin's Contracts and Rights Analyst at (617) 351-3345.

Macromedia and Flash are trademarks or Macromedia, Inc. Macintosh is a registered trademark of Apple Computer, Inc used under license. Windows is a registered trademark of Microsoft Corporation. All other trademarks are the property of their respective owners.

ISBN 0-618-47153-

900

9 780618 471539